The **MAILBOX®**

Calendar Time
for
Little Learners

Keep calendar time fresh, fun, and focused!

- **Transition tips and tunes**
- **Student birthday celebrations**
- **Daily weather assessments**
- **Literacy and math connections**
- **Songs and rhymes**

PLUS ideas for every month of the year!

Managing Editors: Kelly Robertson and Brenda Miner

Editorial Team: Karen Ginn Almond, Becky S. Andrews, Randi Austin, Diane Badden, Kimberley Bruck, Karen A. Brudnak, Marie E. Cecchini, Pam Crane, Roxanne LaBell Dearman, Laura Del Prete, Sarah Foreman, Pierce Foster, Kristin Bauer Ganoung, Deborah Garmon, Karen Guess, Tazmen Hansen, Erica Haver, Marsha Heim, Lori Z. Henry, Debra Liverman, Kitty Lowrance, Jennifer Nunn, Tina Petersen, Gerri Primak, Robyn Pryor, Mark Rainey, Greg D. Rieves, Mary Robles, Hope Rodgers, Rebecca Saunders, Leanne S. Swinson, Donna K. Teal, Rachael Traylor, Sharon M. Tresino, Susan Walker, Carole Watkins, Zane Williard, Virginia Zeletzki

www.themailbox.com

©2010 The Mailbox® Books
All rights reserved.
ISBN10 #1-56234-951-1 • ISBN13 #978-156234-951-6

Printed in the United States
10 9 8 7 6 5 4 3 2 1

HPS 215498

What's Inside

Ideas for any time of year!

- Management tips
- Songs and rhymes
- Literacy skill builders

- Birthday celebrations
- Weather awareness
- Math skill builders

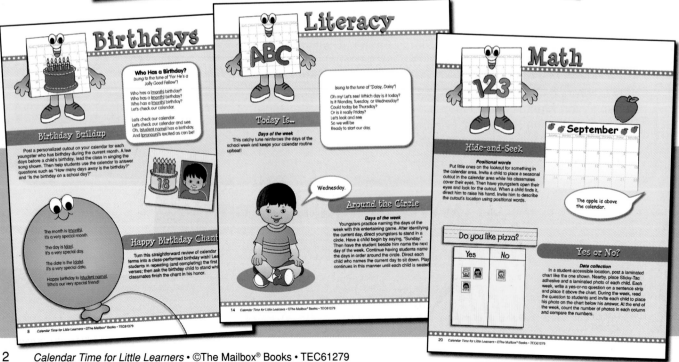

Ideas for each month!

- **A song to welcome the month**
- **Theme-related activities**
- **Celebration ideas**
- **Simple crafts**

Just for November

Welcoming the Month

After leading youngsters in singing this song, invite them to discuss how trees change during the fall.

(sung to the tune of "Row, Row, Row Your Boat")

When it's November,
Leaves on the trees,
Everywhere we look we see
Red, yellow, and brown!

"Leaf-ing" November Behind

Here's a fun way to count the days in November. Post a leafless tree cutout in a location accessible to students. Then use Sticky-Tac adhesive to attach a fall-colored leaf cutout (pattern on page 48) to the tree for each day in November. Each day during calendar time, invite a child to remove a leaf from the tree and post it near the bottom of the tree trunk. (Each Monday, invite additional youngsters to remove leaves for Saturday and Sunday as well.) Then lead the group in counting the leaves that remain on the tree to determine the days left in November. **For an added challenge,** lead students in counting the leaves on the tree and the leaves that have been removed and comparing the amounts.

Calendar Time for Little Learners • ©The Mailbox® Books • TEC61279 45

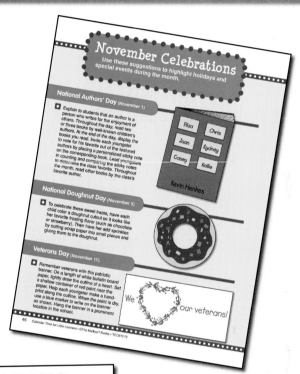

November Celebrations

Use these suggestions to highlight holidays and special events during the month.

National Authors' Day (November 1)

☐ Explain to students that an author is a person who writes for the enjoyment of others. Throughout the day, read two or three books by well-known children's authors. At the end of the day, display the books you read. Invite each child to vote for his favorite by placing a personalized sticky note on the corresponding book. Lead youngsters in counting and comparing the sticky notes to determine the class favorite. Throughout the month, read other books by the class's favorite author.

National Doughnut Day (November 5)

☐ To celebrate these sweet treats, have each child color a doughnut cutout so it looks like her favorite frosting flavor (such as chocolate or strawberry). Then have her add sprinkles by cutting scrap paper into small pieces and gluing them to the doughnut.

Veterans Day (November 11)

☐ Remember veterans with this patriotic banner. On a length of white bulletin board paper, lightly draw the outline of a heart. Set a shallow container of red paint near the paper. Help each youngster make a handprint along the outline. When the paint is dry, use a blue marker to write on the banner as shown. Hang the banner in a prominent location in the school.

46 *Calendar Time for Little Learners • ©The Mailbox® Books • TEC61279*

Just for March

Welcoming the Month

Lead little ones in this toe-tapping tune to familiarize them with March's changing weather. After singing the song, have students determine if the weather outside is like a lion (cold, wet, windy) or like a lamb (warm, sunny, mild). Then attach a lion or lamb cutout to the calendar for that day.

(sung to the tune of "When the Saints Go Marching In")

Oh, March roars in
Like a lion.
The winds are strong as they can be!
But then it leaves so soft and gently
Like a sweet little lamb, you see!

Lucky Days

Post a large pot of gold cutout. Each day of the month, invite a child to attach a gold coin cutout above the pot. (Every Monday have a student attach two extra coins, one for Saturday and one for Sunday, above the pot.) Then lead youngsters in counting the gold coins to determine the current date, how many days are left in the month, and how many days of the month have gone by.

Calendar Time for Little Learners • ©The Mailbox® Books • TEC61279

March Celebrations

Use these suggestions to highlight holidays and special events during the month.

National Nutrition Month (March 1–31)

☐ Cut pictures of different foods (including several healthy and unhealthy choices) from magazines. Place the pictures and a roll of tape near a chart like the one shown. Lead students in a discussion about healthy and unhealthy foods. Then have each child, in turn, choose a picture and show it to the group. Have the class help each youngster decide on which side of the chart to tape the picture.

National Umbrella Month (March 1–31)

☐ Have each child draw on an umbrella cutout a picture of her favorite thing to do on a rainy day. Invite each youngster, in turn, to share her umbrella with the group as she describes the pictured activity.

National Pig Day (March 1)

☐ Celebrate this barnyard animal by having youngsters make pig masks. Have each child color and cut out a copy of the patterns on page 64. Direct him to glue the patterns together as shown; then help him cut out the eyeholes. Finally, help each child tape his project to a jumbo craft stick to complete his mask.

62 *Calendar Time for Little Learners • ©The Mailbox® Books • TEC61279*

Act Happy Week (annually, the week beginning with the third Monday in March)

☐ Have each student share an activity that makes him happy as you write his words on a paper strip. Place the completed strips in a container. Each day during the week, have a few students, in turn, draw a strip and pantomime the activity for his classmates to identify.

riding a bike

St. Patrick's Day (March 17)

☐ In advance, secretly hide a pot of gold cutout in the classroom. Tell students that a sneaky leprechaun hid a pot of gold. Then invite little ones to use magnifying glasses (if desired, make them from green tagboard) to hunt for the leprechaun's gold. After a child finds the gold, reward each student with a small prize, such as a shamrock sticker.

Start of Spring (March 19, 20, or 21)

☐ Celebrate the beginning of spring by having each child make a personalized flower. To make one, a child glues a trimmed photo to the center of a flower cutout. Then she crumples tissue paper squares and glues them to the flower to frame the photo.

Calendar Time for Little Learners • ©The Mailbox® Books • TEC61279 63

Table of Contents

Today's weather is...

Anytime

Catchy Cue

Use this song to signal children to gather for calendar time. Continue singing the song with the group until the last child is seated and ready to begin.

(sung to the tune of
"Row, Row, Row Your Boat")

Stop and listen, please.
Calendar time is here.
Please clean up quietly and gather together.
Starting time is near.

Chant and Clap

To get everyone's attention before calendar time begins, lead students in chanting the name of the current month while clapping out each syllable. Vary the volume of the chant from a whisper (with soft clapping) to a cheer (with enthusiastic clapping).

Friday.

Daily Bop

Calendar time doesn't have to be humdrum! Choose a different movement to correspond to each of the following parts of the calendar: the month, the day, and the date. Encourage youngsters to use the same movements each day for the whole month. For example, lead students in marching as they name the month, twisting as they name the day of the week, and clapping as they count to the number that corresponds to the day's date.

Pick a Stick

To get more students involved in your daily calendar routine, try this! Personalize a craft stick for each child and place the sticks in a decorated container. For each calendar time activity, pick a stick and have that child perform the corresponding task. Continue in the same manner for each remaining task.

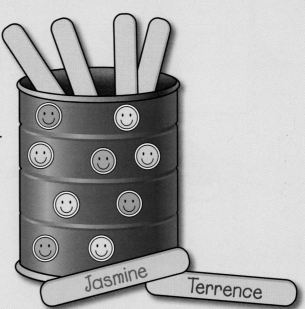

Act It Out

Here's an action-packed way to help youngsters learn the months of the year. Guide students to determine an appropriate action for each month, such as pretending to shovel snow in January or pretending to put on sunscreen in July. Each day during calendar time, lead youngsters in reciting the months of the year in order as they perform the corresponding actions.

Star-Studded Dates

Use this star prop to call attention to special dates during calendar time. To make a prop, cut a star shape from a yellow paper plate or yellow card stock. Then cut a hole in the center of the star and tape a large craft stick to the back of it. To highlight a particular date on the calendar, invite a youngster to find the date and hold the star up to the calendar so the date shows through the hole.

Name animals that live in the ocean.

Calendar Time Tasks

Work daily skills practice into your calendar time routine! On each blank card in a supply, write a task such as "Count to 20," "Say the alphabet," or "Name things that have stripes." Place the cards in a file box. Each day at the beginning of calendar time, invite a child to take a card from the box. Then read the card aloud and guide students in completing the task. As youngsters develop more skills, add new cards to the box.

Missing Date

Each day prior to students' arrival, remove a date cutout from the calendar (or select the cutout for the current date). Then hide the cutout in a student-accessible location. At the beginning of calendar time, ask the group to name the missing date. Then invite a volunteer to find the date and return it to the appropriate place on the calendar.

(sung to the tune of "If You're Happy and You Know It")

If you're happy that it's [day of the week], clap your hands.
If you're happy that it's [day of the week], clap your hands.
If you're happy that it's [day of the week],
If you're happy that it's [day of the week],
If you're happy that it's [day of the week], clap your hands.

A Song of Days

This action song helps students review the days of the week while also getting the wiggles out. If desired, replace *clap your hands* with a different motion each day.

Birthdays

Birthday Buildup

Post a personalized cutout on your calendar for each youngster who has a birthday during the current month. A few days before a child's birthday, lead the class in singing the song shown. Then help students use the calendar to answer questions such as "How many days away is the birthday?" and "Is the birthday on a school day?"

Who Has a Birthday?
(sung to the tune of "For He's a Jolly Good Fellow")

Who has a [month] birthday?
Who has a [month] birthday?
Who has a [month] birthday?
Let's check our calendar.

Let's check our calendar.
Let's check our calendar and see.
Oh, [student name] has a birthday,
And [pronoun]'s excited as can be!

The month is [month].
It's a very special month.

The day is [day].
It's a very special day.

The date is the [date].
It's a very special date.

Happy birthday to [student name],
Who's our very special friend!

Happy Birthday Chant

Turn this straightforward review of calendar terms into a class-performed birthday wish! Lead students in repeating (and completing) the first three verses; then ask the birthday child to stand while his classmates finish the chant in his honor.

Happy Birthday, Emma!

Guess Who!

Invite youngsters to guess who the birthday boy or girl is. On a child's birthday, provide clues, one at a time, about his or her identity. After each clue, invite a volunteer to guess who the featured child is. Once the birthday boy or girl has been correctly identified, hang a sign, similar to the one shown, near the calendar. If it is more than one student's birthday on a given day, repeat the process for each birthday child.

A Special Wand

Make a birthday wand by attaching a cupcake cutout to the end of a pointer. Then invite the child whose birthday it is to use the pointer to help with calendar time. Have him use the wand to point out the current date, to count the number of days left in the month, and to count how many days of the month have gone by. He can also use the wand to point to the month or day of the week and when pointing out today, yesterday, and tomorrow.

Birthday Pictograph

This year-round display serves as a reminder of birthdays and as a tool for teaching simple graphing skills. Write each month on a separate blank card and attach the cards to the wall in a column. For each child, label a cupcake cutout with her name and birthday. After each child decorates her cupcake, attach it to the wall beside the card labeled with the corresponding birthday month. When the graph is complete, discuss the results of the graph with the group. Incorporate the words *more, fewer, most,* and *equal* as appropriate.

Weather

It is sunny and warm outside.

Weather Watcher

In advance, explain to students what a meteorologist does. Each day, invite a different child to pretend to be a meteorologist. Give her a toy microphone and have her stand near a window. Shift the group's attention to the window and have the meteorologist describe the weather conditions outside.

Add a Link

sunny   rainy   snowy   cloudy   windy   foggy

Keep track of daily weather conditions with this graphing idea. Color and cut apart a copy of the weather cards on page 13 and post them in a student-accessible location. Attach a plastic hook under each card. Set a supply of 1" x 6" colorful paper strips and tape nearby. Each day, after observing the weather, have a youngster use a paper strip and tape to make a link to add to the appropriate chain. At the end of the month, count the links in each chain and compare the results.

Take a Look

Share with students that weather conditions can change many times during the day. Place props such as large sunglasses or toy binoculars near a window designated as the weather-viewing area. Invite youngsters to visit the area throughout the day and use one or more of the props to observe the weather conditions. Encourage youngsters to report if the weather conditions have changed.

How's the Weather?

Lead the group in singing this toe-tapping ditty to the daily classroom weather person to encourage him to share his observations.

(sung to the tune of "Clementine")

How's the weather? How's the weather?
Won't you tell us what you see?
Is it sunny? Is it raining?
Oh, tell us, won't you please?

What will tomorrow's weather be?	
Weather	Number of Students
sunny	10
rainy	3
snowy	0
cloudy	4
windy	1
foggy	0

Tomorrow Will Be...

Encourage youngsters to make weather predictions with this activity. Use a copy of the weather cards on page 13 to make a chart like the one shown. Laminate the chart and post it near the calendar. After observing the day's weather, have students predict what tomorrow's weather will be like. Name the different weather conditions and have each child raise his hand when his choice is named. Use a wipe-off marker to record the number of students who choose each weather type. The next day, check the predictions and discuss the results.

Weather

Dressed for the Weather

Gather outerwear and gear for different types of weather and put them in a container. Place the container near the calendar. During calendar time, invite one child to put on the appropriate outerwear and gear for the current weather conditions. Then invite him to explain his choices to the group.

True or False

Today is hot and snowy. False! Help youngsters distinguish true weather observations from false ones with this daily activity. Make a statement about the weather, such as "It is windy today." Then have students look out the window to observe the weather. Invite a volunteer to tell whether your statement is true or false. If the statement is false, have the volunteer make a true statement about the weather.

Tracking the Weather

Use this daily routine to keep a record of the weather conditions for the month. Copy and color a supply of the weather cards on page 13. (If necessary, reduce the size of the cards so they will fit in the date spaces of your calendar.) Each day, have the group observe the weather conditions. Then invite a child to write the date on a corresponding weather card and attach it to the appropriate calendar space. At the end of the month, count each type of weather card and lead youngsters in discussing the results.

September

Sunday	Monday	Tuesday	Wednesday	Thursday	Friday	Saturday
				1 sunny	2 sunny	3 rainy
4 cloudy	5 sunny	6 cloudy				

Use with "Add a Link" on page 10, "Tomorrow Will Be…" on page 11, and "Tracking the Weather" on page 12.

rainy

TEC61279

snowy

TEC61279

cloudy

TEC61279

sunny

TEC61279

windy

TEC61279

foggy

TEC61279

Literacy

Today Is...

Days of the week
This catchy tune reinforces the days of the school week and keeps your calendar routine upbeat!

(sung to the tune of "Daisy, Daisy")

Oh my! Let's see! Which day is it today?
Is it Monday, Tuesday, or Wednesday?
Could today be Thursday?
Or is it really Friday?
Let's look and see
So we will be
Ready to start our day.

Wednesday.

Around the Circle

Days of the week
Youngsters practice naming the days of the week with this entertaining game. After identifying the current day, direct youngsters to stand in a circle. Have a child begin by saying, "Sunday." Then have the student beside him name the next day of the week. Continue having students name the days in order around the circle. Direct each child who names the current day to sit down. Play continues in this manner until each child is seated.

In a Row

Days of the week

This orderly activity gives youngsters practice with an important calendar skill. Label each of seven large cards with a different day of the week. Give each card to a different child and have those youngsters stand in front of the group. Lead the group in reading the cards in the order in which they appear. Then invite volunteers to help arrange the cards in the correct order. After the cards are in order, read them again.

Sunday	Monday	Tuesday	Wednesday	Thursday	Friday

Month Melody

Months of the year

In advance, gather a prop for each month and explain how the prop corresponds to the month. Then invite each of twelve youngsters to hold a prop and stand in front of the group. As the group sings, direct each child to hold up his prop when the corresponding month is named.

(sung to the tune of "Ten Little Indians")

January, February, March, and April,
May, June, July, August, and September,
And then come October, November, and December:
These are the months of the year.

What's in a Name?

Phonological awareness
After singing this song with little ones, lead them in naming the days of the week, emphasizing each beginning and ending sound. Then guide youngsters to realize that some of the days begin with different sounds but that they all end with the same sound.

(sung to the tune of the chorus of "Jingle Bells")

Every day of the week
Has a special name.
Some start out differently,
But they all end the same.

Hop to It

Calendar vocabulary
Use this display to help little ones practice using the words *yesterday, today,* and *tomorrow.* Glue a library pocket to each of seven kangaroo cutouts (pattern on page 19). Label each pocket with a day of the week and label the three blank cards as shown. Attach the kangaroos to tagboard and post the display in a student-accessible location. Set the cards nearby. After discussing the current day of the week, invite a volunteer to place each card in the appropriate pocket.

Looking for Letters

Letter recognition

Your little explorers are sure to enjoy this search for letters. Each day, hide a few letter cutouts in the calendar area. Ask youngsters to imagine they are explorers on a letter hunt. Then name a letter that you hid and invite a volunteer to find it. **For an added challenge,** encourage the child to make the letter's sound or name a word that begins with the letter.

Silly Sentences

Beginning sounds

Review with youngsters the beginning sound of the current month or day. Then invite volunteers to name words that begin with the same sound. Write the words on the board and enlist students' help in using several of the words to make a silly alliterative sentence. **For an added challenge,** have the students say the sentence several times, increasing their speed each time.

Monday
macaroni
muffin
morning
monkey
meatballs
make

Monkeys make meatballs, macaroni, and muffins on Monday mornings.

Personal Stories

Skill review

Each day, choose a skill, such as letter recognition, sight words, capitalization, or punctuation. Use items from the chosen skill to write on chart paper a humorous story about a student. During calendar time, share the story with the group. After reading the story, invite youngsters to use markers to circle each item in the story that is related to the skill.

> ### Jack's Story
>
> One day, Jack was riding his (green) bike. He saw a (red) and (yellow) cow and an alligator wearing a (blue) dress. Then he saw that the grass was (orange) and the sky was (purple). He could not believe his eyes.

I Remember...

Writing

Use this class journal to encourage students to preserve memories. On the last school day of the month, invite each child to draw a picture of a favorite memory from that month. Then have him dictate or write a sentence about his drawing. Bind the papers between two construction paper covers. If desired, also include monthly charts from the calendar, such as the weather graph or the lost tooth chart. Share the journal with the group before placing it in the reading area.

February Memories

A dentist came to our class. He told us how to brush our teeth.

TEC61279

Math

September

Sunday	Monday	Tuesday	Wednesday	Thursday	Friday	Saturday
						1
2	3	4	5	6	7	8
9	10	11	12	13	14	15
16	17	18	19	20	21	22

Hide-and-Seek

Positional words

Put little ones on the lookout for something in the calendar area. Invite a child to place a seasonal cutout in the calendar area while his classmates cover their eyes. Then have youngsters open their eyes and look for the cutout. When a child finds it, direct him to raise his hand. Invite him to describe the cutout's location using positional words.

The apple is above the calendar.

Do you like pizza?

Yes	No

Yes or No?

Data collection

In a student-accessible location, post a laminated chart like the one shown. Nearby, place Sticky-Tac adhesive and a laminated photo of each child. Each week, write a yes-or-no question on a sentence strip and place it above the chart. During the week, read the question to students and invite each child to place his photo on the chart below his answer. At the end of the week, count the number of photos in each column and compare the numbers.

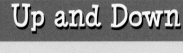

...three, two, one.

Up and Down

Counting

Youngsters practice counting forward and backward while moving their bodies up and down. After the current date has been identified, have youngsters squat in an open area. Beginning with one, lead youngsters in counting to the current date, encouraging them to stand a little taller with each number they say. Then have them count backward from the current date to one, squatting down a little as they say each number.

Count the Caterpillar

Counting

This adorable display grows as it tracks the number of school days that have passed. In a student-accessible location, post a large circle decorated to look like a caterpillar's head. Nearby, place a supply of paper circles, a marker, and Sticky-Tac adhesive. On the first day of school, post a circle labeled with "1" next to the caterpillar's head. Each school day, invite a volunteer to add a consecutively numbered circle to build the caterpillar's body.

Look and Find

Number recognition

This version of I Spy is sure to become a class favorite. Create an "eye-spy" stick by hot-gluing a large wiggle eye to one end of a craft stick. Give a clue, such as "I spy the number five," and ask a volunteer to use the eye-spy stick to point to the number on the calendar. After the class confirms the number choice, give another clue. **For a more challenging game,** present more complex clues, such as "I spy the number that is one less than seven" or "I spy the number that is one more than eight."

Flashlight Fun

Number order

Dim the classroom lights for this kid-pleasing activity. In advance, switch the order of a few date tags on the calendar. At the beginning of calendar time, tell youngsters that the calendar is out of order and enlist their help in fixing it. When a child finds an out-of-order tag, have him raise his hand. Then invite the student to shine a flashlight on the tag and show where it should be moved. Move the tag to that location and continue as described until all the calendar tags are in the right places.

Two Towers

Comparing amounts

Have students predict whether there are more school days or nonschool days during the month. Then place in the calendar area a supply of Unifix cubes in two different colors. Designate one color to represent school days and the other to represent nonschool days. Each school day, have a child add a cube in the appropriate color to make a tower. On the school day following a weekend or holiday, invite a volunteer to add the corresponding number of cubes in the appropriate color to make another tower. At the end of the month, lead youngsters in counting and comparing the two towers and then discuss the results.

Missing Information

Number formation

Use a pencil to write each date of the month on a separate seasonal cutout. Place the resulting date tags and a marker in the calendar area. Each day after the date has been determined, invite a volunteer to trace the date on the corresponding tag. Then help him place the tag in the appropriate calendar space. **For an added challenge,** leave the tags unprogrammed and invite volunteers to write the dates on the tags.

Sunday	Monday	Tuesday	Wednesday	Thursday	Friday	Saturday
						1
2	3	4	5	6	7	8
9	10	11	12	13	14	15

October

Coin Stew

Counting coins

Stir up some coin-counting fun by adding this activity to your daily calendar routine. To make coin stew, place a few imitation coins in a small cup and set a spoon nearby. During calendar time, invite a volunteer to determine the value of the coin stew. Have her use the spoon to stir the coin stew and then help her count the coins and write the amount on the board. Change the number of coins each day.

Two, four, six, eight, ten,...

Calendar Cover-Up

Number recognition, counting by twos

This simple idea provides practice with two skills. Name an odd number and invite a volunteer to use a small sticky note to cover the matching date on the calendar. Continue in this manner until all the odd numbers are covered. Guide students to notice that every other number is covered. Tell little ones that the remaining numbers are the ones used to count by twos. Then lead students in counting by twos by pointing to each remaining number, in order, and leading the group in saying its name.

Sunday	Monday	Tuesday	Wednesday	Thursday	Friday	Saturday
	2		4		6		8
		10		12		14	
16		18		20		22

August

A Big Load

Place value

To make a truck, label a 9" x 12" sheet of construction paper as shown. Also color and cut out a copy of the truck pattern on page 26. Glue the cutout and three construction paper wheels to the labeled paper. Then laminate the project for durability and post it near the calendar. Keep a supply of sticky notes labeled for tens and ones nearby. Each day have a student adjust the truck's cargo so it equals the day's date.

More Fries, Please!

Place value

For a tasty way to keep track of how many days of school have passed, try this! Gather three different-size fry containers from a fast food restaurant and label them as shown. Place the containers in the calendar area and set yellow tagboard strips (fries) and rubber bands nearby. Each day, add a fry to the "ones" container and lead youngsters in counting the fries in the container. Then guide students to help you adjust the positions and groupings of the fries as needed, bundling groups of ten or 100 with rubber bands. Finally, count the fries to reveal how many school days have passed.

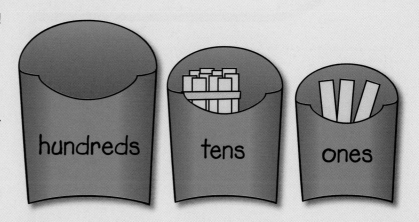

Truck Pattern
Use with "A Big Load" on page 25.

TEC61279

Calendar Time for Little Learners • ©The Mailbox® Books • TEC61279

Monthly Booklet-Making Activity

Pages 27–32

How to use the booklet:

Each month, guide students in making a booklet to review and discuss the current month. Then use each child's completed booklets to assess his progress throughout the year.

How to prepare the booklet:

1. Program a copy of pages 28–31 with the current month; then copy each page to make a class supply.
2. Give each child a copy of pages 28–31. Also give each child who has a birthday in the current month a copy of page 32.
3. Help each child stack his pages in order between two construction paper covers and staple the booklet along the top.

How to complete the booklet:

1. Help each child write his name and the current month on his booklet cover; then have him decorate the cover as desired.
2. Refer to the directions at the bottom of each page to guide students in completing the page.

month

Sunday	Monday	Tuesday	Wednesday	Thursday	Friday	Saturday

Calendar Time for Little Learners • ©The Mailbox® Books • TEC61279

Note to the teacher: Have a student decorate the sides of the page with drawings or stickers that correspond with the month. Then help him number the days of the month. If desired, have the child find specific dates and ask him to color, cross out, or circle the corresponding calendar square. (For example, say, "Find the first Monday of the month. Color it yellow.")

month

first name

last name

me

my favorite things

Calendar Time for Little Learners • ©The Mailbox® Books • TEC61279

Note to the teacher: Have each child practice writing his name on a sheet of writing paper. Then have him copy his best example on the page. Invite him to add illustrations of himself and of a few of his favorite things.

What Happened This Month

month

What I Think Will Happen This Month

Calendar Time for Little Learners • ©The Mailbox® Books • TEC61279

Note to the teacher: At the beginning of the month, read the text in the left thought bubble aloud. Have each student draw or write to predict something that will happen during the month. At the end of the month, read the text in the other thought bubble aloud and have the child write or draw about something that happened during the month. Lead students in discussing their predictions and whether they were correct.

month

Sunblock

Happy New Year

Calendar Time for Little Learners • ©The Mailbox® Books • TEC61279

Note to the teacher: Invite each child to color the symbols that she thinks correspond with the current month. When students are satisfied with their work, lead them in a discussion about the reasons they chose the symbols.

Happy birthday to me!

My name is _____.

My birthday is _____.

I am _____ years old.

Calendar Time for Little Learners • ©The Mailbox® Books • TEC61279

Note to the teacher: Help each child whose birthday is in the current month write his name, birthday, and age on the page. Then have him draw the appropriate number of candles on the cake and decorate it as desired.

Just for August

Welcoming the Month

Lead youngsters in singing this song. Next, guide them in saying the dates on the calendar, beginning with "one." Then invite a volunteer to name the current date.

(sung to the tune of "Twinkle, Twinkle, Little Star")

August, August,
School is in—
Time for learning to begin.
Calendars are so much fun.
August starts with number one.
Tell me, tell me.
Who can say
What number comes next today?

Picnic Time!

Use this display to track how many days have gone by during the month of August. In a student-accessible location, post a construction paper picnic blanket like the one shown. Set a black marker nearby. Each day, invite a volunteer to draw an ant on the picnic blanket. (On Mondays, also have volunteers draw ants for the previous Saturday and Sunday.) Then have the group count the ants on the blanket to determine how many days of the month have gone by.

One, two, three, four, five!

August Celebrations
Use these suggestions to highlight holidays and special events during the month.

National Inventors' Month (August 1–31)

This robot walks the dog.

- Spark students' creativity while helping them understand the importance of inventions. Near the beginning of the month, lead students in a discussion about inventions. Encourage volunteers to name some examples. Then invite each child to draw an invention of his creation on a lightbulb cutout. Also have him dictate a sentence about his invention for you to write on his cutout. Each day during the month, invite a few youngsters to tell about their inventions. If desired, post the lightbulbs on a board titled "Bright Ideas."

National Watermelon Day (August 3)

- Post a large seedless watermelon slice cutout in a student-accessible location. Set a black ink pad nearby. Give each child a sample of watermelon to taste. Then gather the group near the watermelon cutout. In turn, invite each child to press a fingertip on the ink pad and make a fingerprint (seed) on the watermelon as she tells something about watermelon. Continue until each child has added a seed.

Happiness Happens Day (August 8)

- Encourage youngsters to share things that make them happy. Hold a smiley face cutout as you sit in a circle with youngsters. To begin, name something that makes you happy. Then pass the smiley face to the child next to you and invite her to share something that makes her happy. Continue passing the smiley face around the circle until each child has shared.

I like to build sand castles.

Leah

National Relaxation Day (August 15)

○ Explain to youngsters that to relax, people sometimes participate in favorite activities. Invite youngsters to brainstorm relaxing activities as you list them on the board. Then have each child dictate or write a sentence about her favorite relaxing activity and then illustrate it. Bind the completed pages together to make a class book titled "How to Relax."

National Banana Split Day
(August 25)

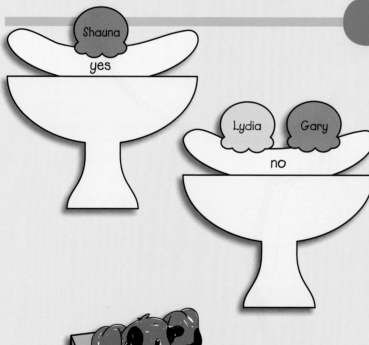

Shauna
yes

Lydia   Gary
no

○ Use these yummy treats to learn about student preferences. Prepare a personalized ice cream scoop for each child. Also make two large bowl cutouts and two banana cutouts. Write *yes* on one banana and *no* on the other; then arrange the bowls and bananas on the floor as shown. Ask students a yes-or-no question, such as "Do you like ice cream?" and invite each youngster to place his scoop above the banana that matches his answer. Count and compare the scoops on the banana splits. Remove the scoops and repeat the process with a different question.

National Dog Day (August 26)

Skippy

○ To make an adorable dog puppet, have each child color and cut out the patterns on page 36. Invite her to dictate the name of her dog for you to write on the tag. Then have her make a puppet like the one shown by gluing the patterns to a paper lunch bag. Encourage each child to use her puppet to tell the class one thing she knows about dogs.

Dog Puppet Patterns
Use with "National Dog Day" on page 35.

Calendar Time for Little Learners • ©The Mailbox® Books • TEC61279

Just for September

Welcoming the Month

Use this lively song to signal the start of calendar time and to familiarize little ones with the name of the month. Each time youngsters sing the word *September*, use a pointer or your hand to underscore the word on your calendar.

(sung to the chorus of "Jingle Bells")

September, September,
September's here, hooray!
I'm at school
To make new friends
And to listen, learn, and play!

Munchin' Through the Month

This cute visual reminds students that September comes and then it goes! Use a red marker to draw the outline of a large apple on white bulletin board paper. Color a stem, a worm, and several seeds; then cut out the shape. When displaying the cutout, secure only the midsection (from top to bottom) and keep the cutout within your students' reach. Each September day before students depart, invite a child to gently tear a "bite" from the apple (symbolizing that a part of September has passed). By the month's end, only a core will remain!

Day by Day

Keep calendar skills up-to-date during September with this little ditty. After singing the song with the class, ask a volunteer to name the current day and show the current date on the calendar.

(sung to the tune of "Three Blind Mice")

September! September!
School has begun. We're having fun!
Let's look for today on the calendar.
Find the day and the date on the
  calendar.
Who is ready to come to the calendar?
Please raise your hand.

A Tale of Three Apples

Build a better sense of time sequence with three apple cutouts. Cut the apples and leaves from colorful paper. Program the leaves as shown (use the terms "Before Today" and "After Today" with younger students) and glue them in place. Then hot-glue a wooden clothespin stem to each apple. As part of your calendar routine, clip to each apple an item that represents the time frame.

September Celebrations

Use these suggestions to highlight holidays and special events during the month.

Labor Day (annually, the first Monday in September)

- Throughout the month, have little ones perform different career-related actions, such as directing traffic as a police officer or delivering mail as a mail carrier.

National Grandparents Day (annually, the first Sunday after Labor Day)

- Teach students the song shown about one week before the holiday. During calendar time, have students count the number of days until the holiday and rehearse the song for their loved ones.

I Love You!
(sung to the tune of "Where Is Thumbkin?")

I love [Grandma/Grandpa].
I love [Grandma/Grandpa].
Yes, I do!
[She/He] loves me too!
I'll give [her/him] hugs and kisses
And many happy wishes
On Grandparents Day, Grandparents Day.

Constitution Day and Citizenship Day (September 17)

- Have each child make a stars and stripes headband to wear during calendar time on Constitution Day and Citizenship Day. Then lead the group in singing a familiar patriotic tune.

September

National Play-Doh Day (September, day varies)

- The brightly colored modeling clay for children was introduced in the mid 1950s. To celebrate, give each child a clump of colorful clay to mold and shape during the day. Invite students to showcase their sculptures at a chosen classroom location.

Start of Fall (September 22 or 23)

- People all over the world have roughly 12 hours of daylight and 12 hours of darkness on the first day of fall in the northern hemisphere. Use a circle cutout that is half yellow (for sunlight) and half black (for darkness) to mark this special day on your calendar. Have each child illustrate her favorite fall activity.

Johnny Appleseed's Birthday (September 26)

- This poem is a perfect pick for introducing the legend of Johnny Appleseed. Show students THANK YOU in sign language (see illustration) and then invite them to sign the phrase during the poem and throughout the day!

Thank you, Johnny Appleseed,
For planting all those apple seeds
That grew and grew
Into big apple trees.

Thank you, Johnny Appleseed,
For your generosity.
Your birthday is
A special day to me.

Just for October

Welcoming the Month

Sing this song to introduce October. Then invite students to describe what October means to them. Record youngsters' responses on a large leaf or pumpkin cutout. Post the cutout and continue to add comments to it throughout the month.

(sung to the tune of "Head and Shoulders")

October is when leaves fall from trees.
October is when leaves swirl around.
It's when we pick pumpkins, orange
    and round,
From vines on the ground, on the ground!

Where's the Leaf?

Place three different-colored leaf cutouts (yellow, red, and orange) near your calendar. A few times a week, display each leaf on a different calendar date. Then ask calendar-related questions about the placement of the leaves, or give clues about the placement of each leaf and invite youngsters to answer the questions or identify the locations of the leaves.

Find the yellow leaf. Is it on a school day? How do you know?

October Celebrations

Use these suggestions to highlight holidays and special events during the month.

National Pizza Month (October 1–31)

- Make a large pizza shape like the one shown and display it for the group. Each day of the month, invite a child to attach a red circle (pepperoni) to the pizza. (Every Monday have a student attach two extra pepperonis to the pizza: one for Saturday and one for Sunday.) Then lead youngsters in counting the pepperonis to determine the current date, how many days are left in the month, and how many days of the month have gone by.

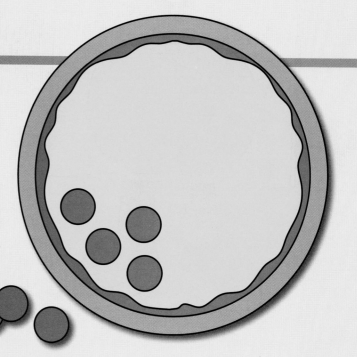

National Popcorn Poppin' Month
(October 1–31)

- Display a large popcorn cutout, labeled as shown. Give some popcorn to each child and ask him to use his senses to explore the popcorn. Write students' observations about the popcorn in the appropriate sections of the cutout.

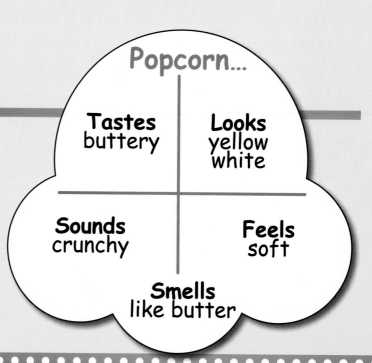

Popcorn...

Tastes buttery

Looks yellow white

Sounds crunchy

Feels soft

Smells like butter

Columbus Day (annually, the second Monday in October)

- Tell students that Christopher Columbus was an explorer who lived long ago. Explain that he wanted to discover new places. Have youngsters see what they can discover in the classroom by playing a calendar-related game of I Spy.

Fire Prevention Week
(annually, the Sunday through Saturday period in which October 9 falls)

Make a fire escape plan for your family.

- Cut seven paper squares to fit your calendar spaces. On one side of each square, draw a flame. On the flip side of each square, write a fire safety rule. Post the squares (flame side up) on the calendar spaces that coincide with Fire Prevention Week. Each day, turn over the corresponding flame, read the rule aloud, and encourage little ones to talk about it. (On Monday, also share Sunday's rule; on Friday, also share Saturday's rule.) For added fun, wear a firefighter's hat during the activity.

National School Bus Safety Week
(annually, the third full week in October)

School Bus Safety
- Stay seated—Abby
- Talk quietly—Marcus
- Listen to the driver—James

- Lead youngsters in discussing school bus safety. Then invite each child, in turn, to share a way that she can be safe when riding on a school bus. Record students' responses on a large school bus cutout.

October

National Character Counts Week
(annually, the third week in October)

- Introduce your students to Likable Lyle, a chosen puppet that always demonstrates good character traits. Each day of the week, use Likable Lyle to lead students in a discussion about a different character trait.

National Candy Corn Day
(October 30)

- Have each child make a candy corn stick puppet like the one shown. Then lead young-sters in singing the song. Encourage students to wave their puppets in the air each time they sing the words *candy corn.*

  (sung to the chorus of "Jingle Bells")

  Oh, candy corn, candy corn,
  It's a yummy treat!
  Bits of yellow, orange, and white,
  So tasty and so sweet!
  Candy corn, candy corn,
  It's a special day,
  So let's eat this yummy treat
  And smile and shout, "Hooray!"

Halloween (October 31)

- Use a jack-o'-lantern cutout to mark the date on your calendar. Invite students to describe their favorite family traditions for this spooky holiday!

Just for November

Welcoming the Month

After leading youngsters in singing this song, invite them to discuss how trees change during the fall.

*(sung to the tune of
"Row, Row, Row Your Boat")*

When it's November,
Leaves fall to the ground.
Everywhere we look we see
Red, yellow, and brown!

"Leaf-ing" November Behind

Here's a fun way to count the days in November. Post a leafless tree cutout in a location accessible to students. Then use Sticky-Tac adhesive to attach a fall-colored leaf cutout (pattern on page 48) to the tree for each day in November. Each day during calendar time, invite a child to remove a leaf from the tree and post it near the bottom of the tree trunk. (Each Monday, invite additional youngsters to remove leaves for Saturday and Sunday as well.) Then lead the group in counting the leaves that remain on the tree to determine the days left in November. **For an added challenge,** lead students in counting the leaves on the tree and the leaves that have been removed and comparing the amounts.

November Celebrations

Use these suggestions to highlight holidays and special events during the month.

National Authors' Day (November 1)

- Explain to students that an author is a person who writes for the enjoyment of others. Throughout the day, read two or three books by well-known children's authors. At the end of the day, display the books you read. Invite each youngster to vote for his favorite out of the featured authors by placing a personalized sticky note on the corresponding book. Lead youngsters in counting and comparing the sticky notes to determine the class favorite. Throughout the month, read other books by the class's favorite author.

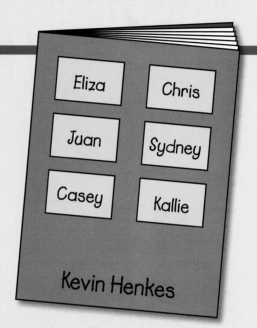

National Doughnut Day (November 5)

- To celebrate these sweet treats, have each child color a doughnut cutout so it looks like her favorite frosting flavor (such as chocolate or strawberry). Then have her add sprinkles by cutting scrap paper into small pieces and gluing them to the doughnut.

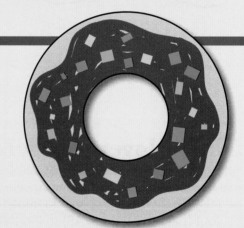

Veterans Day (November 11)

- Remember veterans with this patriotic banner. On a length of white bulletin board paper, lightly draw the outline of a heart. Set a shallow container of red paint near the paper. Help each youngster make a handprint along the outline. When the paint is dry, use a blue marker to write on the banner as shown. Hang the banner in a prominent location in the school.

American Education Week
(week prior to the week of Thanksgiving)

◉ Play charades to celebrate all the wonderful things about school. Each day of the week, have a few students, in turn, act out their favorite school activities. As each child performs, invite the group to guess the activity he is acting out. Choose the next performer, ensuring that each child has had a turn by the end of the month.

I Love to Write Day (November 15)

◉ On this day people of all ages are encouraged to write. Invite your youngsters to write to share some of their favorite things. Have each child think of a favorite animal, toy, or activity and write or dictate to tell about her choice. Have her add an illustration to her writing before sharing it with the group.

Polar bears are my favorite animals.

Thanksgiving Day (fourth Thursday in November)

◉ Students will gobble up some Thanksgiving fun while wearing these adorable headbands. Have each child color and cut out a copy of the turkey pattern on page 48. Direct her to glue craft feathers to the back of the turkey's body. Then have her glue the completed turkey to a sentence strip. Size each child's sentence strip to fit her head and staple it to complete the headband. Encourage youngsters to wear their headbands as they perform Thanksgiving songs and poems.

Leaf Patterns
Use with "'Leaf-ing' November Behind" on page 45.

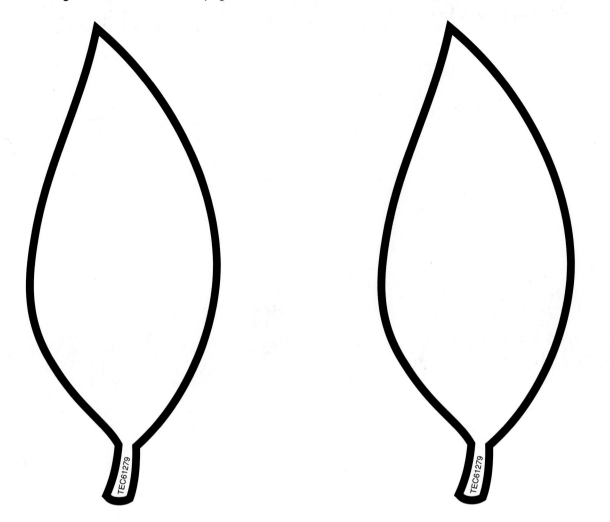

Turkey Pattern
Use with "Thanksgiving Day" on page 47.

Calendar Time for Little Learners • ©The Mailbox® Books • TEC61279

Just for December

Welcoming the Month

Use this song to introduce the weather changes that December brings. After leading youngsters in singing the song, draw a T chart on the board. Invite youngsters to name things they like and dislike about December's weather as you write their responses on the chart.

(sung to the tune of "I'm a Little Teapot")

December is the last month of the year.
It's when wintertime's finally here.
There are so many things that we can do.
We can sled and build snowmen too.

How Many Days?

Help little ones count down to the start of winter break! Program a large seasonal cutout as shown. Then staple a paper link to it for each school day until winter break begins. Each school day during December, ask a volunteer to remove a link from the chain. Then lead the group in counting the remaining links and reciting the poem on the cutout, inserting the corresponding number. Continue until all the links have been removed.

Winter break
Is in [number of links] days.
We'll ring in the fun
In special ways!

December's Gift

Attach 31 gift bows to a large gift box cutout and post the cutout near your calendar. Each day, invite a child to remove a bow from the gift and set it aside. (Every Monday have a student remove two additional bows, one for Saturday and one for Sunday.) Then lead youngsters in counting the remaining bows to determine how many days are left in the month.

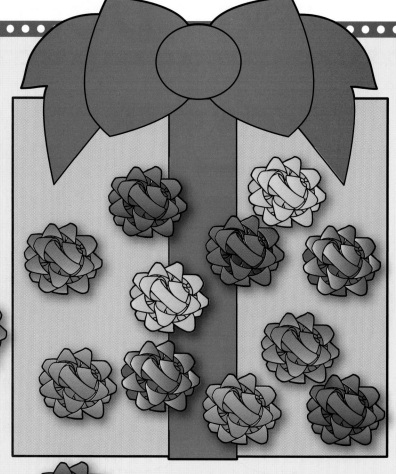

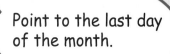

Point to the last day of the month.

22	23	24	25	26	27	28
29	30	31				

Here and There

Move this sweet little guy around the calendar to review a variety of skills. To make a gingerbread man pointer, attach a craft stick to a gingerbread man cutout. During calendar time, invite volunteers to use the pointer to highlight items such as the date for yesterday, today, tomorrow, or the first or last day of the month.

December Celebrations

Use these suggestions to highlight holidays and special events during the month.

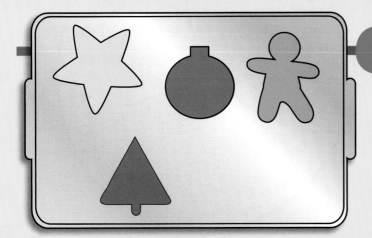

National Cookie Day (December 4)

- To celebrate this tasty occasion, set out play dough, rolling pins, cookie cutters, and cookie sheets. Encourage youngsters to roll out the play dough and cut cookie shapes from it. Then have them place their cookies on the cookie sheets to "bake" them. After cleaning up the play dough cookies, give each child a real cookie to eat.

Poinsettia Day (December 12)

- Share the beauty of this festive flower with your little ones. Display a picture of a poinsettia and invite volunteers to name words that describe it. Write each descriptive word on a separate card and then post the cards around the poinsettia.

Hanukkah (begins Kislev 25 of the Hebrew calendar and lasts for eight days)

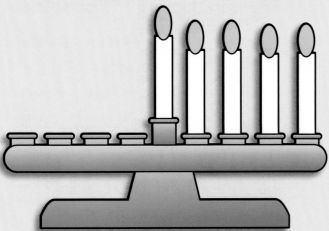

- Post a menorah cutout and set nine candle cutouts, nine flame cutouts, and Sticky-Tac adhesive nearby. On the first day of Hanukkah, invite a volunteer to attach the shammash (center candle) and one other candle to the menorah. Then have him "light" the menorah by attaching a flame over each candle, beginning with the shammash. At the end of the school day, remove the flames to ready the menorah for the next day. Each day add an additional candle and flame to correspond with the days of Hanukkah.

December

Winter Solstice (December 21 or 22)

- In the northern hemisphere, this day begins the winter season. It also falls on or near the longest night of the year. Prepare a moon cutout similar to the one shown. Invite each child, in turn, to hold the moon cutout and share an activity that he does at night.

Christmas (December 25)

- Throughout the month, invite a few youngsters each day to wear Santa hats. Have each Santa watch for classmates who are demonstrating exceptional behavior. At the end of the day, ask each Santa to share the names of classmates who he thinks should be added to Santa's nice list.

Kwanzaa (December 26–January 1)

- To encourage the Kwanzaa principle of kuumba (creativity), set out a variety of art materials, such as clay, paint, craft sticks, and pom-poms. Have each child use the materials to make a gift for a friend or family member. Encourage him to share his finished project with the group.

Just for January

Welcoming the Month

Ring in a new month and a new year with this toe-tapping tune! Lead youngsters in singing the song. Then explain that, at the beginning of January, people make resolutions about things they would like to accomplish during the new year. Invite each youngster to share a resolution.

(sung to the tune of "Yankee Doodle")

January is the month
That starts a brand-new year.
It is the month when we wish
Our friends good health and cheer.

January is the month
When we all start new,
Making promises to do
Good things the whole year through.

Perky Penguins

Enlist youngsters' help in setting up the calendar for the month. Write each number from 1 to 31 on a separate penguin cutout (patterns on page 56). Place the penguin labeled with "1" in the appropriate calendar space. Hide the remaining cutouts around the classroom. Have little ones find the penguins. Then invite each child to waddle to the calendar and help him place his penguin in the correct space on the calendar.

❄ ❄ ❄ ❄ January ❄ ❄ ❄ ❄						
Sunday	Monday	Tuesday	Wednesday	Thursday	Friday	Saturday
			🐧1	🐧2	🐧3	🐧4

Gathering Snowballs

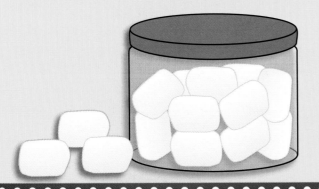

Practice counting skills with this cool idea. Place a clear container in your calendar area and set a supply of cotton balls (snowballs) nearby. Each day, invite a youngster to place a snowball in the container. At the end of the month, lead students in counting the snowballs to determine the number of school days in January.

January Celebrations

Use these suggestions to highlight holidays and special events during the month.

National Soup Month (January 1–31)

- Gather students in a circle and place a large pot and spoon in the middle. In turn, invite each youngster to stir the imaginary soup in the pot as he names a kind of soup he likes to eat. Write each student's response on a large soup-pot cutout.

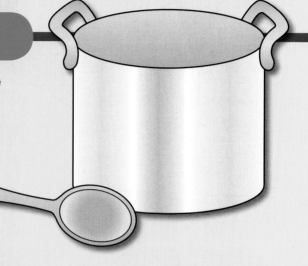

International Creativity Month (January 1–31)

- Encourage youngsters to use their creativity to think of imaginative ways to use common classroom items. Throughout the month, show students different items, such as a pencil or a paper clip. Guide little ones to brainstorm unique ways to use each item.

Put lots of paper clips together to make a necklace.

Bend a paper clip to make a hook.

New Year's Day (January 1)

- Invite each child to wear a paper party hat. Then lead students in counting backward from ten. As youngsters say each number, have them squat a little lower. When they reach the number one, invite them to jump up and say with a cheer, "Happy New Year!"

Happy New Year!

Ways to Be Kind

I will help clean up. Laura
I will help a friend who is hurt. Sophie
I will not say mean things. Austin

Martin Luther King Day (annually, the third Monday in January)

- Remind youngsters that Martin Luther King Jr. wanted people to be kind and helpful to one another. Then have students stand in a circle and join hands. Invite each child to name a way he can be kind or helpful to his classmates. Write students' responses on a large heart cutout labeled as shown. After each child has shared, post the heart in the classroom.

Chinese New Year (annually, can begin between January 21 and February 21)

- Let good fortune dance through your classroom with a dragon parade. Prepare a large dragon head cutout (enlarge the dragon pattern on page 56). Give each child two crepe paper streamers and have him hold one in each hand. Hold the dragon head and direct students to line up behind you. As you lead youngsters around the room, encourage them to dance and wave the streamers.

Mmmm, chocolate pie.

National Pie Day (January 23)

- Enlist youngsters' help in brainstorming a list of pie flavors. Then hold a disposable pie pan and sit in a circle with your students. Pretend to smell the imaginary pie as you say, "Mmmm, [apple] pie." Pass the pan to the student beside you. Invite her to imitate your actions, but encourage her to name a different flavor of pie she would like to eat. Continue until each child has had a turn.

Penguin Patterns
Use with "Perky Penguins" on page 53.

Dragon Pattern
Use with "Chinese New Year" on page 55.

Welcoming the Month

Lead youngsters in singing this song at the beginning of February to introduce the groundhog's role in predicting the weather. Then invite little ones to make their own predictions about upcoming weather conditions.

(sung to the tune of "I've Been Working on the Railroad")

February is when the groundhog
Pops up from the ground.
First, it rubs its sleepy eyes.
Then it looks all around.
If it doesn't see its shadow,
Spring is on its way.
But if the groundhog sees its shadow,
Spring's still six weeks away.

Looking for Hearts

Place three different-colored heart cutouts (red, pink, and white) near your calendar. A few times a week, display each heart on a different date. Then ask calendar-related questions about the placement of the hearts and invite youngsters to answer the questions. Or give clues about the placement of each heart and have students identify the locations of the hearts.

Find the red heart. Is it on a holiday? If so, which one?

February Celebrations

Use these suggestions to highlight holidays and special events during the month.

American Heart Month (February 1–28)

- Tell youngsters that it is important for them to take care of their hearts. Explain that one way to take care of their hearts is to exercise. Have each student place his hand on his heart to feel it beat. Then direct each child to run in place for a few moments. At your signal, have him stop running and feel his heartbeat again. Lead youngsters in discussing how their hearts beat differently when they are at rest as compared to when they are exercising. Guide students to realize that exercising gets their hearts pumping faster, which helps make them healthy and strong.

National Black History Month (February 1–28)

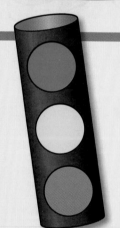

- Throughout the month, discuss several African Americans who have made contributions to our country. Choose one day to discuss Garrett Morgan, the inventor of the stoplight, and invite youngsters to make stoplights. To make one, a child paints a cardboard tube black. When the paint is dry, he glues a red, a yellow, and a green circle to the tube, as shown.

National Children's Dental Health Month (February 1–28)

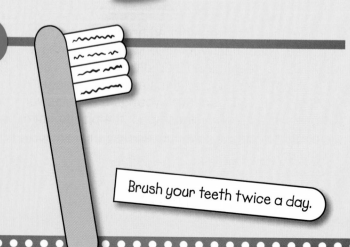

- Cut a large toothbrush handle shape (without bristles) from bulletin board paper. Then round the corners of white paper strips so they look like bristles. Display the toothbrush handle. Periodically throughout the month, write a dental hygiene tip on a bristle and share the tip with the class. Then attach the bristle to the toothbrush handle as shown.

Brush your teeth twice a day.

National Cherry Month (February 1–28)

- Label three containers as shown and set them in a student-accessible location. Give each child a red pom-pom (cherry). Name a food made with cherries. Then invite each youngster to share his feelings about the featured food by placing his cherry in the appropriate container. Lead students in counting the cherries in each container and comparing the amounts. Redistribute the cherries to repeat the process with a different food.

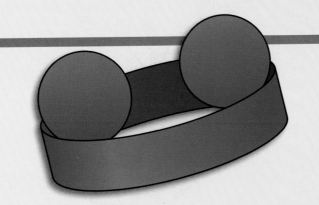

Groundhog Day (February 2)

- Have youngsters make and wear groundhog headbands like the one shown. Then plan to take students outdoors. Before going outside, have your little groundhogs predict whether they will see their shadows. Then take youngsters outside to check their predictions. When you return to the class-room, lead students in a discussion about their predictions and the results.

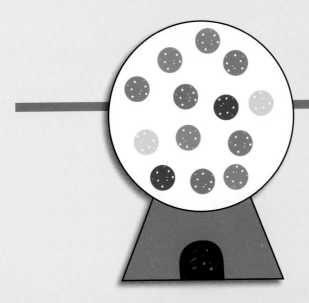

Bubble Gum Day (annually, the first Friday in February)

- Make these adorable gumball machines to celebrate this sticky treat. For each child, glue a white paper circle to a construction paper base as shown. Have each youngster use bingo daubers to make several prints (gumballs) on the circle.

February

Valentine's Day (February 14)

- To make this partner game, program pairs of heart cutouts with valentine messages, such as "Love," "My Friend," or "Be Mine." Then place the hearts at a center. Invite students to arrange the hearts facedown and play a traditional game of Concentration.

Presidents' Day (annually, the third Monday in February)

- Observe Presidents' Day with a game of Follow the Leader. Begin by telling youngsters that a president leads the people who live in his country. Then, in turn, invite each child to be the president. Direct her to make simple movements for her classmates (citizens) to imitate.

National Tooth Fairy Day (February 28)

- Have each child write or dictate a response to the question "What does the tooth fairy do with the all the teeth she collects?" Then have each child illustrate his response. Bind the completed pages between two covers to make a class book.

She uses teeth to make jewelry.

Just for **March**

Welcoming the Month

Lead little ones in this toe-tapping tune to familiarize them with March's changing weather. After singing the song, have students determine if the weather outside is like a lion (cold, wet, windy) or like a lamb (warm, sunny, mild). Then attach a lion or lamb cutout to the calendar for that day.

(sung to the tune of
"When the Saints Go Marching In")

Oh, March roars in
Like a lion.
The winds are strong as they can be!
But then it leaves so soft and gently
Like a sweet little lamb, you see!

Lucky Days

Post a large pot of gold cutout. Each day of the month, invite a child to attach a gold coin cutout above the pot. (Every Monday have a student attach two extra coins, one for Saturday and one for Sunday, above the pot.) Then lead youngsters in counting the gold coins to determine the current date, how many days are left in the month, and how many days of the month have gone by.

March Celebrations

Use these suggestions to highlight holidays and special events during the month.

National Nutrition Month (March 1–31)

- Cut pictures of different foods (including several healthy and unhealthy choices) from magazines. Place the pictures and a roll of tape near a chart like the one shown. Lead students in a discussion about healthy and unhealthy foods. Then have each child, in turn, choose a picture and show it to the group. Have the class help each youngster decide on which side of the chart to tape the picture.

National Umbrella Month (March 1–31)

- Have each child draw on an umbrella cutout a picture of her favorite thing to do on a rainy day. Invite each youngster, in turn, to share her umbrella with the group as she describes the pictured activity.

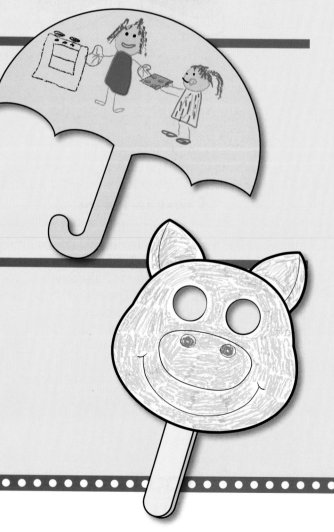

National Pig Day (March 1)

- Celebrate this barnyard animal by having youngsters make pig masks. Have each child color and cut out a copy of the patterns on page 64. Direct him to glue the patterns together as shown; then help him cut out the eyeholes. Finally, help each child tape his project to a jumbo craft stick to complete his mask.

Act Happy Week (annually, the week beginning with the third Monday in March)

- Have each student share an activity that makes him happy as you write his words on a paper strip. Place the completed strips in a container. Each day during the week, have a few students, in turn, draw a strip and pantomime the activity for his classmates to identify.

riding a bike

St. Patrick's Day (March 17)

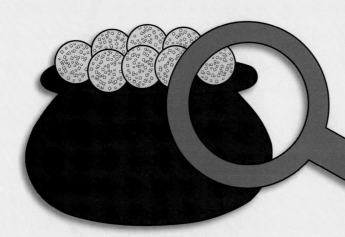

- In advance, secretly hide a pot of gold cutout in the classroom. Tell students that a sneaky leprechaun hid a pot of gold. Then invite little ones to use magnifying glasses (if desired, make them from green tagboard) to hunt for the leprechaun's gold. After a child finds the gold, reward each student with a small prize, such as a shamrock sticker.

Start of Spring (March 19, 20, or 21)

- Celebrate the beginning of spring by having each child make a personalized flower. To make one, a child glues a trimmed photo to the center of a flower cutout. Then she crumples tissue paper squares and glues them to the flower to frame the photo.

Pig Mask Patterns

Use with "National Pig Day" on page 62.

TEC61279

Just for April

Welcoming the Month

Lead youngsters in singing this song to introduce them to some of the wonderful things that begin to happen during April.

(sung to the tune of "Twinkle, Twinkle, Little Star")

April is a month in spring.
Flowers bloom and robins sing.
Gentle rains begin to fall,
Grass and flowers growing tall.
Way up in the bright blue sky,
You might see a butterfly.

Rainy Days

April showers bring May flowers! To keep track of April's rainy days, post an umbrella cutout labeled as shown. Set small raindrop cutouts and tape nearby. Each day, invite youngsters to observe the weather. If it is raining have a volunteer tape a raindrop near the umbrella. At the end of the month, lead youngsters in counting the raindrops to determine the number of rainy days in April.

Rainy Days in April

A Basket of Eggs

Review a variety of calendar skills with this "egg-cellent" idea. On each of several slips of paper, write a calendar task, such as "Point to the first day of the month" or "Count the number of days that have passed this month." Place each slip in a separate plastic egg and put the eggs in a basket. During calendar time, invite a few volunteers to each take an egg. Help each child read the slip and then have him complete the task.

Point to yesterday's date.

Stylish Umbrellas

Highlight important dates with this idea. Set paper drink umbrellas and tape in the calendar area. During the month, when a special day such as a holiday, a birthday, or a field trip day occurs, have a volunteer tape an umbrella to the corresponding date. At the end of the month, revisit the dates and discuss what special happening occurred on that day.

April Celebrations

Use these suggestions to highlight holidays and special events during the month.

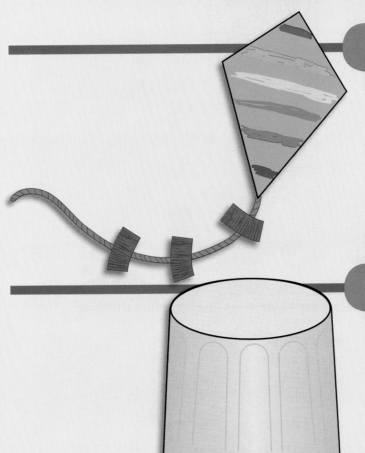

National Kite Month (April 1–30)

- Turn your art center into a kite-making area. To make a kite, a child traces a tagboard kite on a sheet of paper and cuts out the tracing. Then she decorates her kite as desired. To complete her kite, she tapes a yarn tail to its back and crepe paper strips (bows) to the tail. If desired, invite youngsters to pretend to fly their kites outside on a windy day.

April Fools' Day (April 1)

- Prior to students' arrival, make some silly changes to your classroom, such as switching the month on the calendar, scrambling center items, or turning an empty trash can upside down. When students arrive, play a game of April Fools' Day I Spy. Invite youngsters to name the things that have been changed. After all the changes have been named, enlist youngsters' help in getting the room back in order.

National Library Week (annually, the second full week in April)

- Show students several examples of bookmarks. Place a class supply of 2" x 6" tagboard strips in your art center. To make a bookmark, a child decorates a strip as desired. Collect the finished bookmarks and donate them to a local library.

National Jelly Bean Day (April 22)

- Place an equal number of jelly beans in each of two containers of different sizes and shapes, similar to the ones shown. Invite youngsters to study the containers and then to guess which one has more jelly beans. After each child has shared his prediction, reveal to the group that the containers actually have the same number of jelly beans in them. Guide students to conclude that the sizes and shapes of the containers make it appear that one has more jelly beans in it than the other.

Earth Day (April 22)

- These projects are perfect for encouraging youngsters to take care of the earth. After discussing the importance of recycling, have each child use blue and green crayons to color a paper plate so it resembles the earth. Help her fold three paper arrow cutouts as shown and glue them on the plate to make the recycling symbol. Punch a hole in the top and attach a ribbon loop for hanging.

National Dance Day (April 29)

- To celebrate this day devoted to boogying, use a recording of upbeat music. At the end of calendar time, play the music and invite youngsters to perform their favorite dance moves.

Just for May

Welcoming the Month

Lead little ones in singing this toe-tapping tune to introduce a popular May pastime—gardening! Then invite youngsters to name something they would like to grow in a garden. Write students' responses on a large vegetable or flower cutout.

(sung to the tune of "Up on the Housetop")

In May, we watch our garden grow
From seeds planted row by row.
Water them and hope there is lots of sun.
Gardening is so much fun!

Plant, plant, plant,
Row by row,
Watch that garden really grow.
In May, we watch our garden grow
From seeds we planted row by row.

Picking Flowers

This garden helps track the number of days that have gone by in May and also the number of days that are left. To prepare a garden, stand 31 artificial flowers in a block of floral foam. Place a plastic vase or jar nearby. Each school day in May, have a volunteer pick a flower from the garden and place it in the vase. (On Mondays, have volunteers pick flowers for the previous Saturday and Sunday as well.) Lead students in counting the flowers in the vase and in the garden. Then ask questions about the number of flowers in each.

May Celebrations

Use these suggestions to highlight holidays and special events during the month.

National Hamburger Month (May 1–31)

- During the month of May, turn your dramatic-play area into a hamburger stand. Place in the area cookie sheets (for cooking surfaces), aprons, plastic food, empty condiment bottles, plastic plates, and utensils. A child visits the center and pretends to cook hamburgers for customers.

National Smile Month (May 1–31)

- Take a photo of each child smiling and saying, "Cheese!" In the classroom, post a sign similar to the one shown. Each day, lead youngsters in singing the song shown. At the end of the song, attach a student's photo to the sign. Continue the activity daily until each child's photo has been on the sign.

Smile of the Day

(sung to the tune of "If You're Happy and You Know It")

If you're happy and you know it, please say, "Cheese."	*Say, "Cheese!"*
If you're happy and you know it, please say, "Cheese."	*Say, "Cheese!"*
If you're happy and you know it, then your face can't help but show it.	*Smile.*
If you're happy and you know it, please say, "Cheese."	*Say, "Cheese!"*

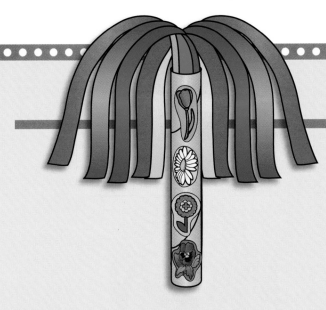

May Day (May 1)

- Invite each child to make a personal maypole. To make one, she cuts pictures of flowers from magazines and glues them to a cardboard tube. Then she cuts (with help) crepe paper into thin strips and tapes one end of each strip to the inside of the tube.

Mother Goose Day (May 1)

- On each of several white feather cutouts, write the name of a Mother Goose rhyme; place the feathers in a basket. Throughout the day, invite a volunteer to take a feather from the basket. Read aloud the name of the rhyme and invite little ones to join you in reciting the rhyme.

"Hickory, Dickory, Dock"

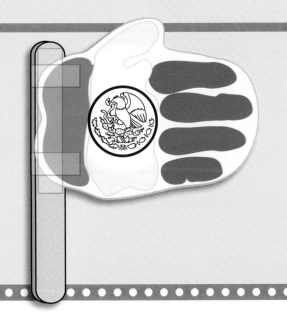

Cinco de Mayo (May 5)

- Show youngsters a picture of the Mexican flag and invite them to name the colors. Then help each child make a replica of the flag by painting his hand with wide stripes of green, white, and red. Have him press his hand on a white index card. When the paint is dry, trim around the handprint and glue a copy of a Mexican flag symbol pattern from page 80 in the center of the white section. Then tape a craft stick to the handprint cutout.

May

Mother's Day (annually, the second Sunday in May)

○ For each child, fold a sheet of white construction paper in half. Unfold the paper and, with a pencil, lightly write *MOM* on the top half. Have each child paint over the word with a thin paintbrush. Then have her fold the paper and gently press down on the top of it. Carefully unfold the paper and allow the paint to dry. To complete her card, each child adds drawings and signs her name.

National Transportation Week (annually, the week including the third Friday in May)

○ Create a display that shows sky, land, and water. Invite each youngster to cut from a magazine a picture of a type of transportation. (If desired, provide clip art instead of magazine pictures.) Then have him show the group his picture and tell something about that form of transportation. Help him glue the picture to the display in an appropriate position.

Memorial Day (annually, the last Monday in May)

○ The poppy is known as the flower of remembrance. Have each child glue together four red paper hearts, a black paper circle, and a green paper stem to make a poppy like the one shown. Encourage youngsters to wear their poppies on Memorial Day.

Just for June

Welcoming the Month

Get youngsters excited about the end of the school year and the beginning of summer break with this catchy tune. (If your school year ends in May, substitute *May* for *June* in the song.) After leading students in singing the song, invite volunteers to name things they would like to do during summer break.

*(sung to the tune of
"If You're Happy and You Know It")*

June is when our school is over for the year.
June is when we know that summertime
    is near.
We will play out in the sun and have lots and
    lots of fun.
We are glad the month of June is finally here.

Sunny Days

Use this visual aid to count the days in June. In a student-accessible location, post a large yellow circle (sun). Set 30 yellow paper strips (rays) and Sticky-Tac adhesive nearby. Each school day, invite a volunteer to attach a ray to the sun. (On Mondays, have volunteers attach rays for the previous Saturday and Sunday.) Then lead the group in counting the rays to determine how many days in June have gone by.

June Celebrations

Use these suggestions to highlight holidays and special events during the month.

National Candy Month (June 1–30)

○ On each of several blank cards, attach clip art of a different type of candy or a familiar candy wrapper. Place the cards faceup in a pocket chart. Have students close their eyes while a child removes one card from the chart. Signal for youngsters to open their eyes and lead them in saying the rhyme below as the child pretends to nibble his candy. Then invite a volunteer to name the missing candy. Return the card to the chart to play another round.

Candy, candy, such a treat.
Which one did [child's name] eat?

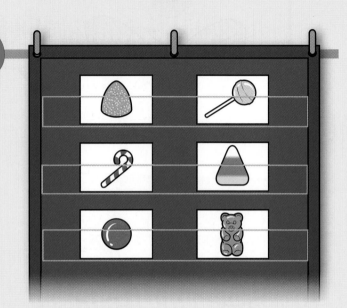

National Dairy Month (June 1–30)

○ Display these adorable cows to celebrate the delicious products made with milk. For each child, cut a slit across the bottom of each of two small white paper cups. To make a cow, a child colors the cups (legs) and a paper plate half (body).Then she colors a cow face cutout (patterns on page 76) and glues it to the body. After she glues a paper strip (tail) to the body, help her slip the plate through the slits in the cups as shown.

(sung to the tune of "Three Blind Mice")

Red, white, blue.
Red, white, blue.
See how it flies.
See how it flies.
Our flag is a symbol
We honor today.
It waves for us,
So we're here to say,
"We love our country,
The U.S.A."
Red, white, blue.
Red, white, blue.

Flag Day (June 14)

Display an American flag and discuss the colors with youngsters. Then have each child color a flag cutout (pattern on page 76) and tape a craft stick to the back to make his own flag. Invite youngsters to wave their flags as you lead them in singing the song shown.

Father's Day (annually, the third Sunday in June)

For each child, prepare a tie-shaped card like the one shown. Encourage each youngster to decorate the front of the card as desired. Then, on the inside, have her write or dictate a personal message to a special man in her life. Finally, have her sign her name.

Summer Begins (annually; June 20, 21, or 22)

In the northern hemisphere, this day marks the beginning of the summer season. Have youngsters sit in a circle. Give a small sun cutout to a child and invite him to tell the group something he likes to do during summer. Then have him pass the sun to the child beside him. After each child has shared, place the sun cutout on the calendar to mark this special day.

I like to play in the pool.

Cow Face Patterns

Use with "National Dairy Month" on page 74.

Flag Pattern

Use with "Flag Day" on page 75.

TEC61279

Just for July

Welcoming the Month

Lead youngsters in singing this song to introduce them to some of the fun activities that occur during July.

(sung to the tune of "My Bonnie Lies Over the Ocean")

July is the month in the summer
For picnics and big parades too.
Fireworks light up the night sky.
There's so much to see and to do.

Beach Ball Bounce

Use this prop to highlight the day of the week. Attach a craft stick to a small beach ball cutout. "Bounce" the beach ball above each day as you lead youngsters in saying the days of the week. Then invite a child to bounce the beach ball on the current day.

July Celebrations

Use these suggestions to highlight holidays and special events during the month.

National Ice Cream Month (July 1–31)

- Have each child color a personalized ice cream scoop cutout (pattern on page 80) to match his favorite ice cream flavor. Place the colored scoops in a clean ice cream container. Post a large cone cutout in a student-accessible location and set the scoops nearby. Each day read the name on a scoop. Invite that child to share her favorite ice cream flavor and then attach her scoop above the cone. Continue until each child's scoop has been added to the cone.

National Hot Dog Month (July 1–31)

- Prepare a graph like the one shown. Invite each child to color a copy of a hot dog card from page 80 to show whether he prefers ketchup, mustard, both, or neither on his hot dog. Then invite him to tape his card to the matching column of the graph. After all the cards have been added to the graph, lead the group in discussing the results. Incorporate the words *more*, *fewer*, *most*, *fewest*, and *equal* as appropriate.

International Joke Day (July 1)

What runs but never walks? Water.

- Adults and children alike can't help but laugh on this day. Several times during the day, read aloud a few jokes from a children's joke book. Near the end of the day, invite youngsters to share the jokes from the day that are their favorites.

Independence Day (July 4)

- To prepare, cut excess film from laminated projects into strips. To make a firecracker, a child paints a cardboard tube red, white, or blue and sets it aside to dry. He uses glitter glue to draw designs on three strips of laminating film. Then help him staple a yellow star cutout to one end of each strip. When the glue is dry, help him staple each strip inside the tube as shown.

National Lollipop Day (July 20)

Five.

- Have little ones stand in a circle. Then give a child a lollipop cutout or a large wrapped lollipop. Announce a number. The child holding the lollipop says, "One" and pretends to lick it once. Then she passes the lollipop to the youngster beside her, who says, "Two," and pretends to lick the lollipop twice. Direct the group to continue counting, pretending to lick the lollipop, and passing the lollipop until the designated number is named. To play another round, announce a different number.

Mexican Flag Symbol Patterns
Use with "Cinco de Mayo" on page 71.

Scoop Pattern
Use with "National Ice Cream Month" on page 78.

Hot Dog Cards
Use with "National Hot Dog Month" on page 78.

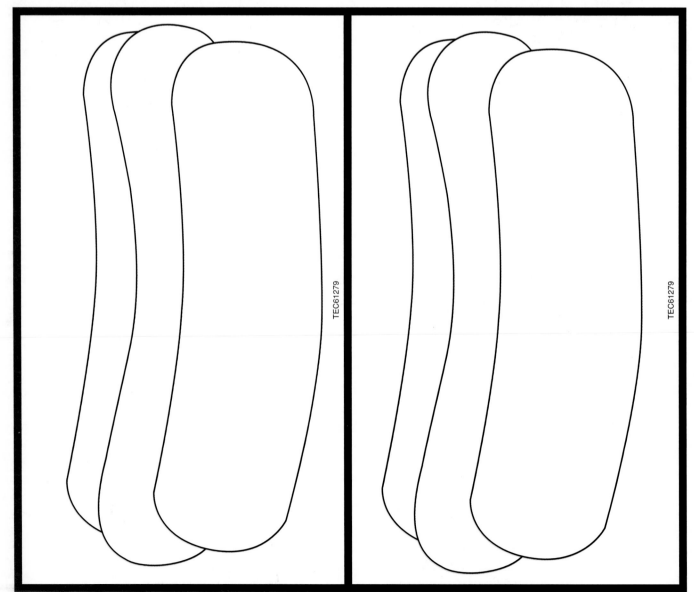